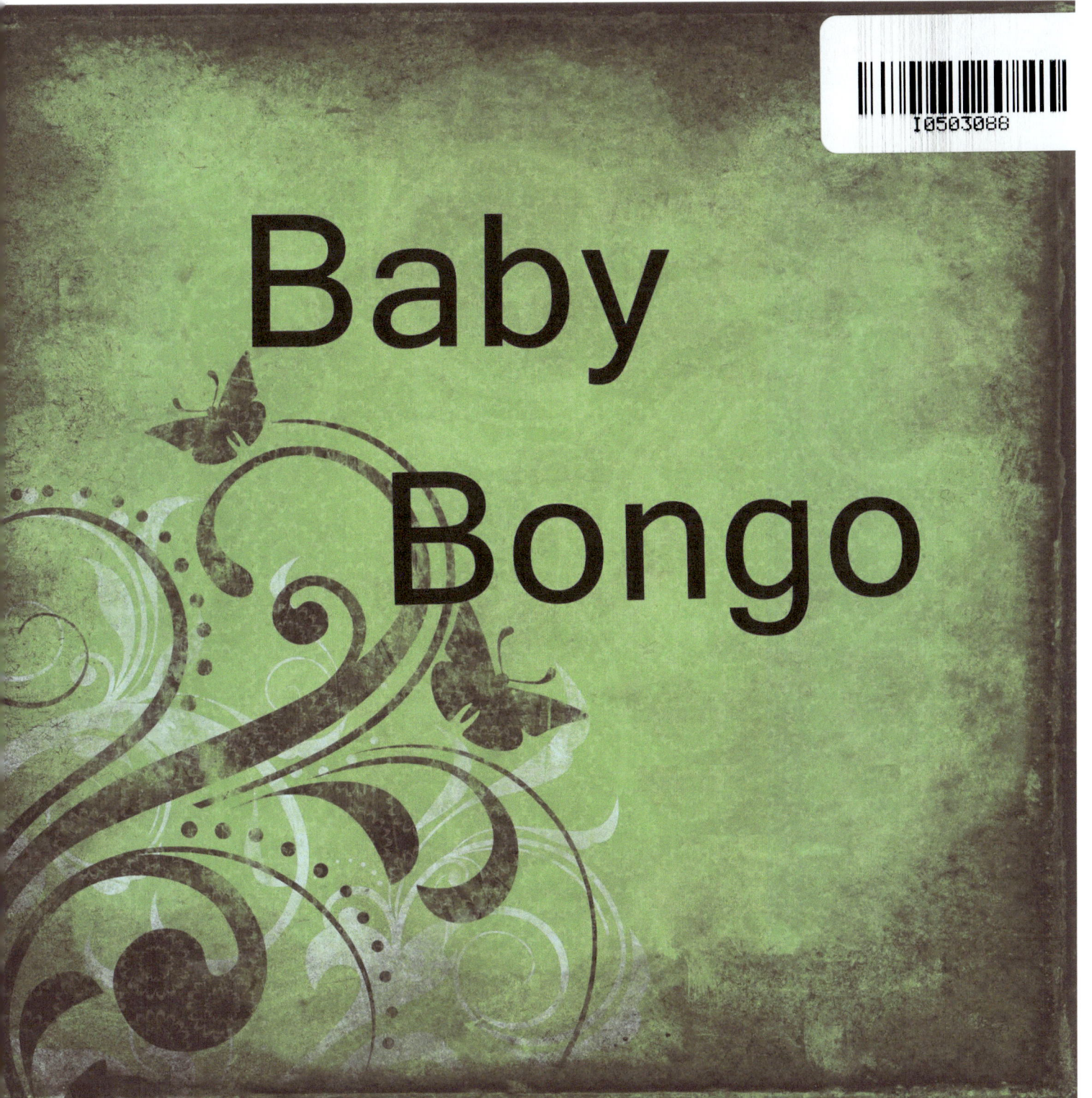

Baby

Bongo

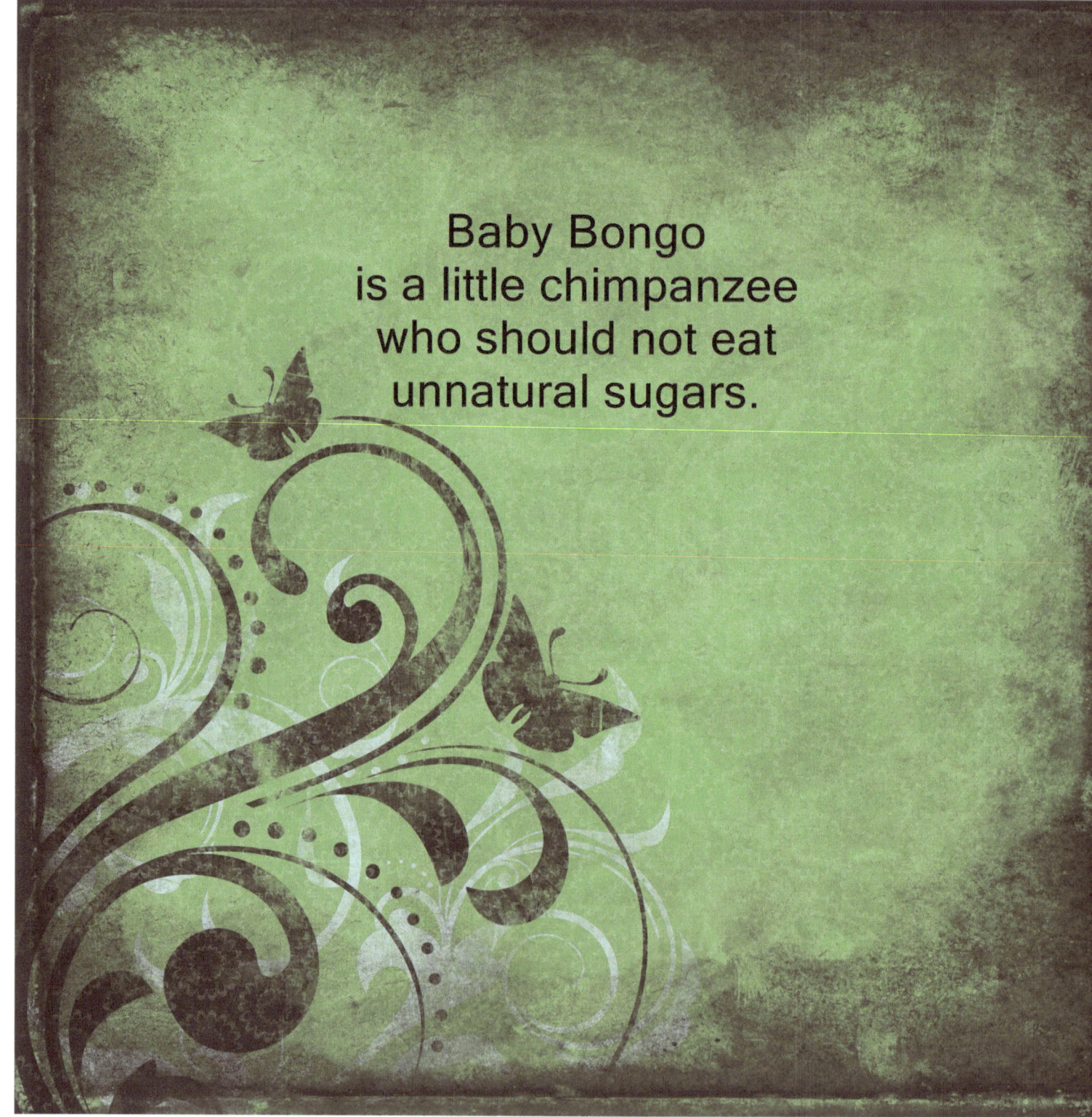

Baby Bongo
is a little chimpanzee
who should not eat
unnatural sugars.

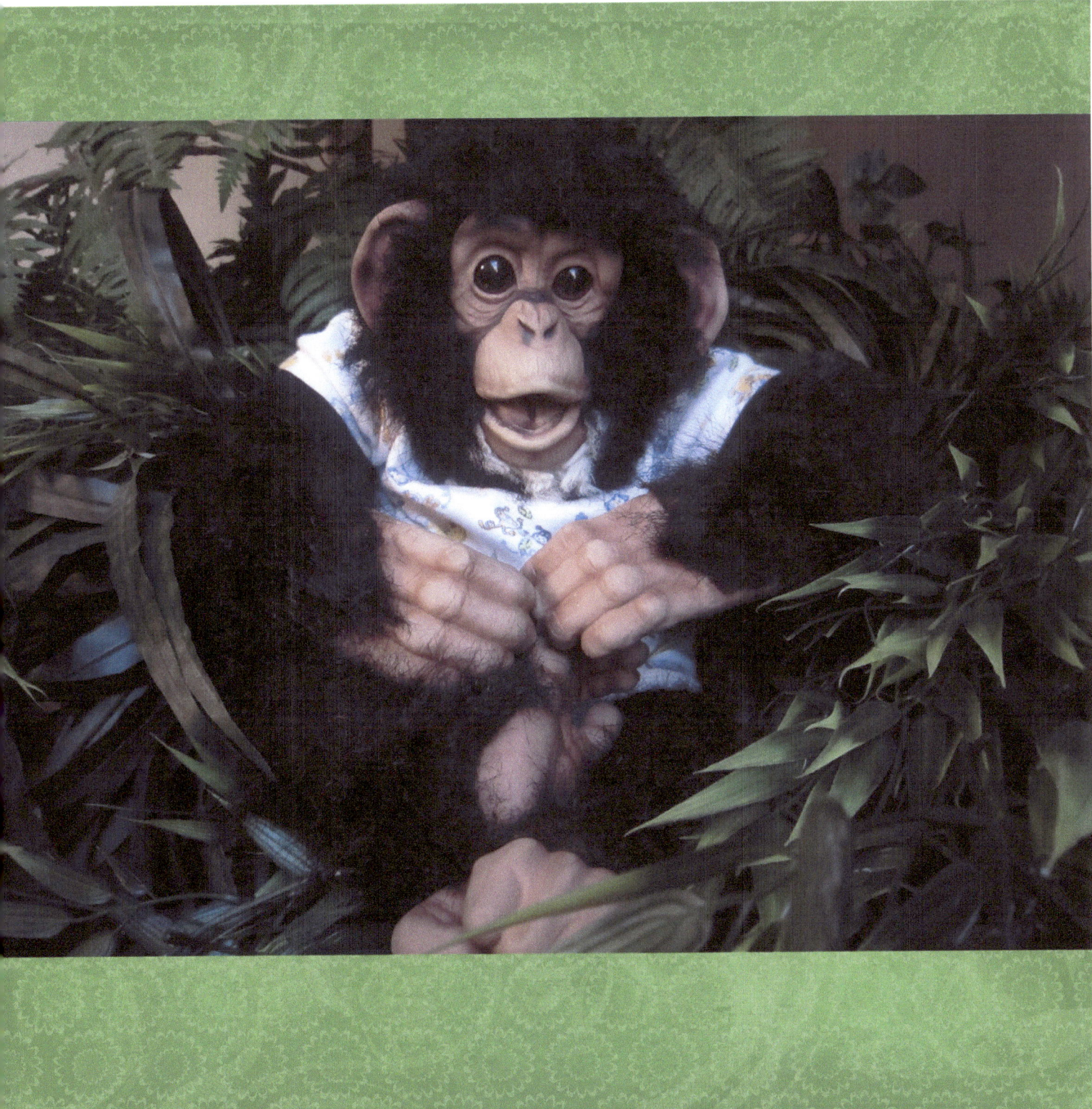

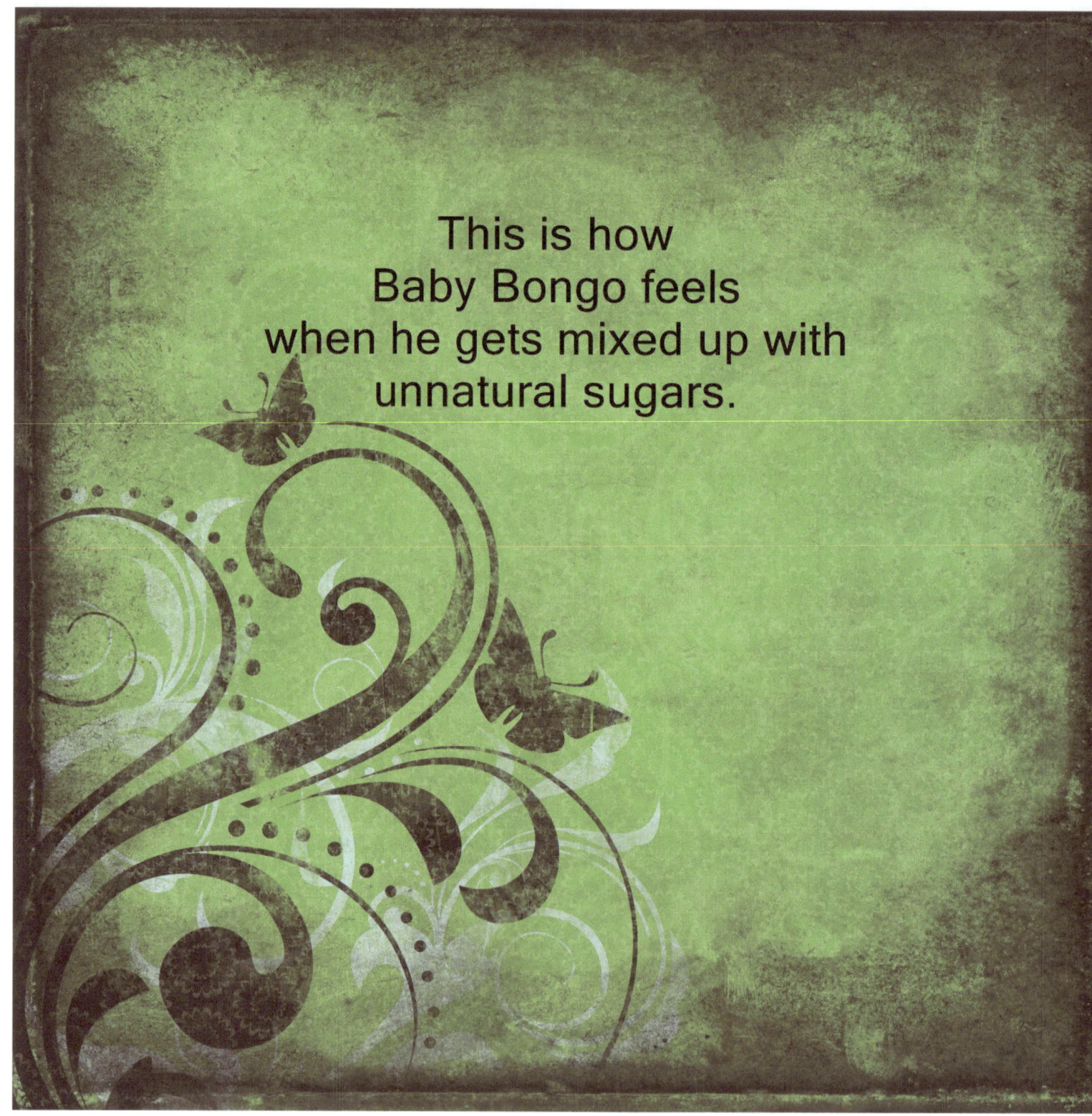

This is how
Baby Bongo feels
when he gets mixed up with
unnatural sugars.

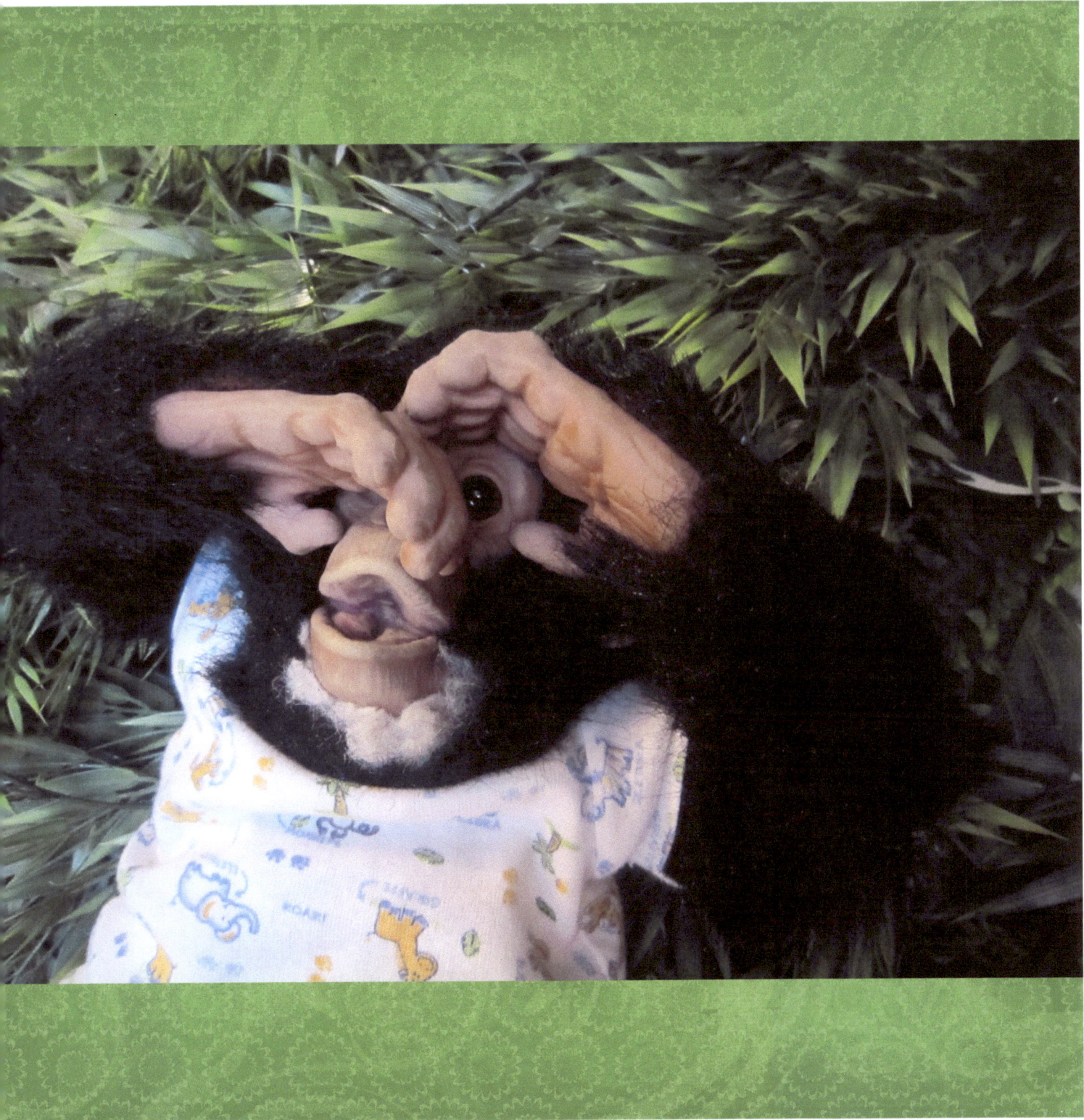

One afternoon Baby Bongo
hid a big yellow box of
sugary donuts in
a secret hiding spot.

Baby Bongo did not want
to tell his Mommy and Daddy
that he had a secret.

His parents had no idea of
what would happen next.

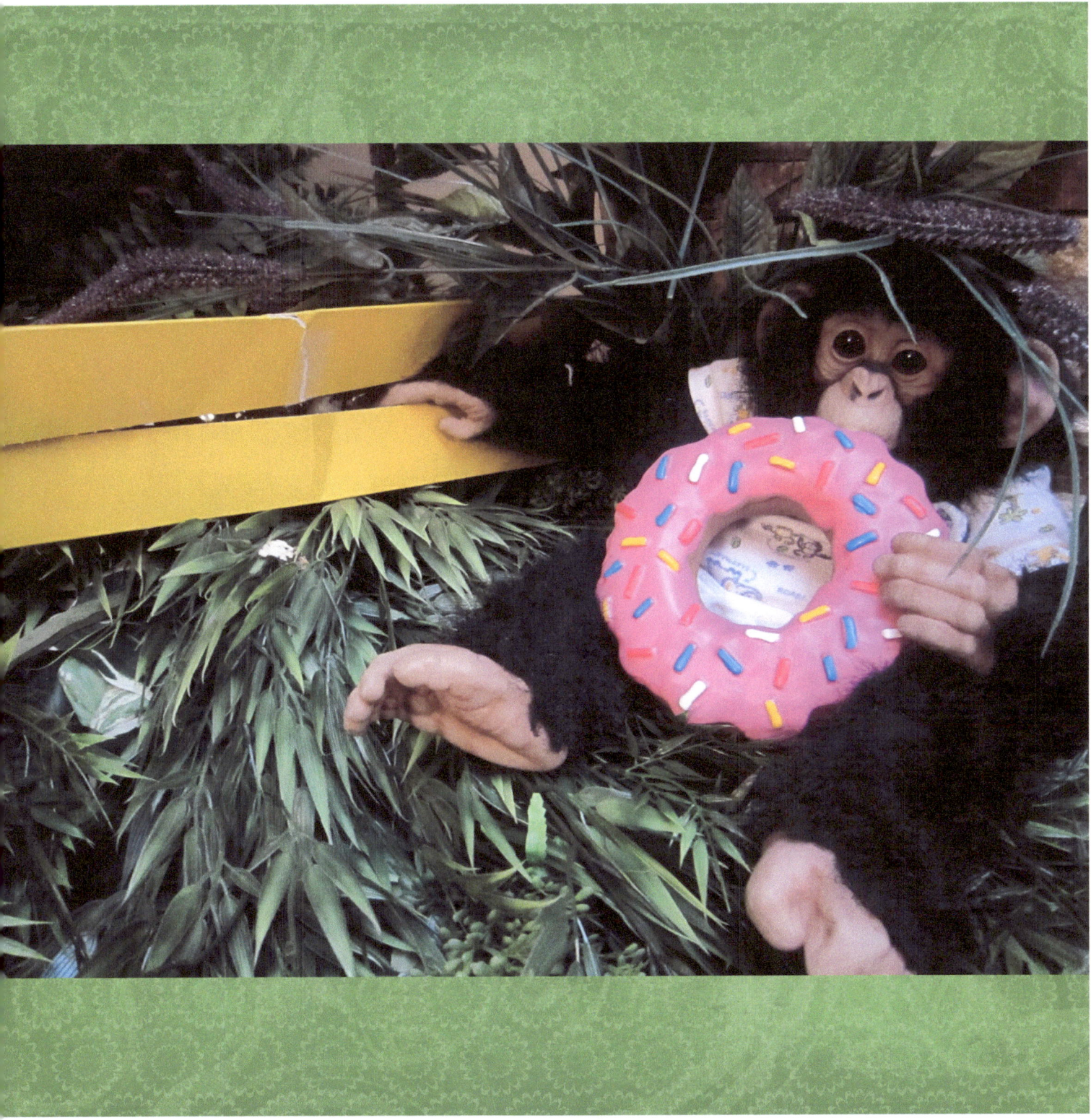

"Time to practice our music lessons,
Baby Bongo" his parents would sing out.

Of course, Baby Bongo would listen,
drumming along with his Mommy and
Daddy in the Baby Bongo Band.

He was focusing on being the instrument
and letting the music flow,
when suddenly Baby Bongo
took a water break.

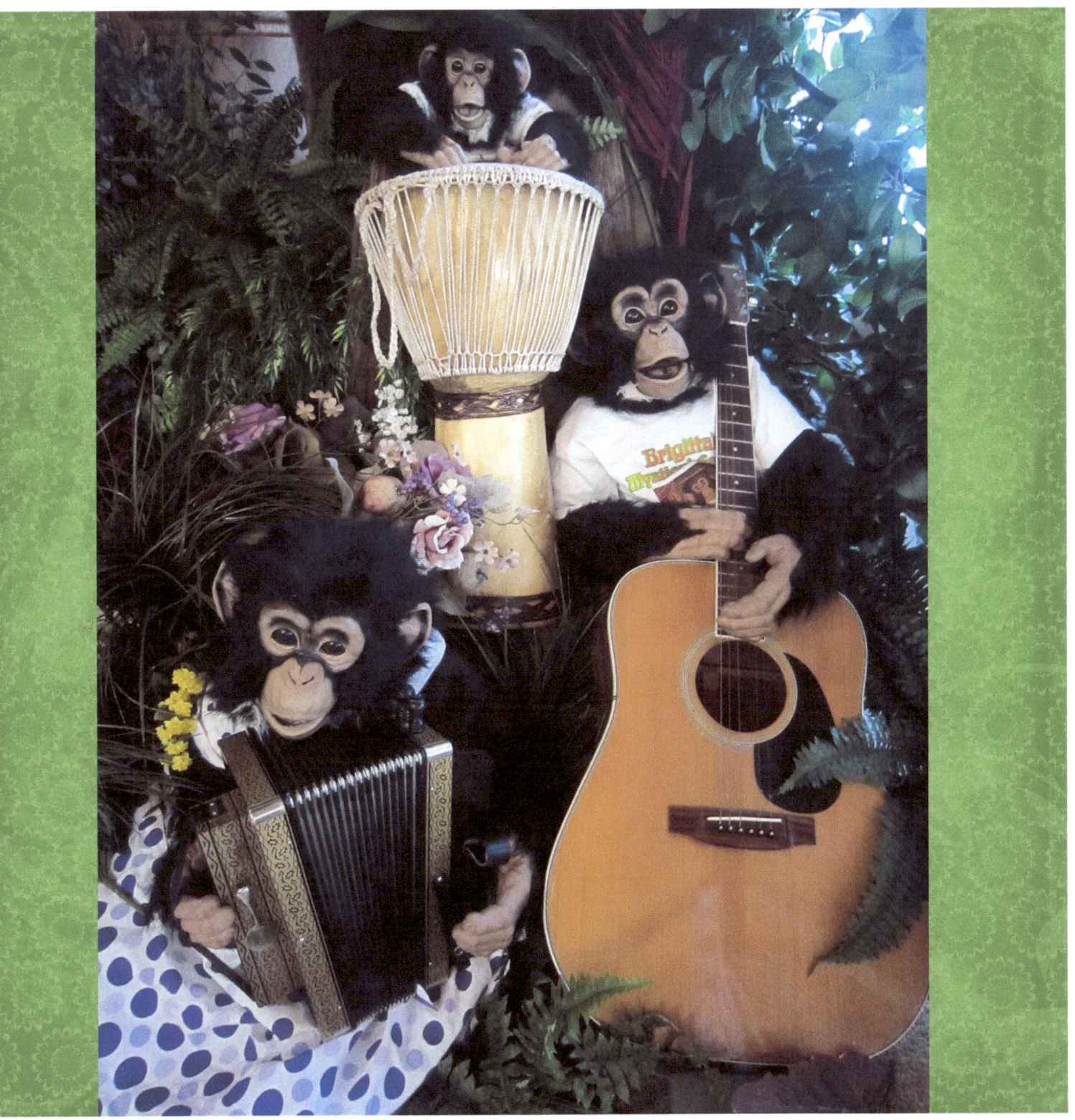

However, instead of
a healthy drink of water,
Baby Bongo hid in
his secret hiding spot
and began to eat all the
sugary donuts he had
found earlier at the playground.

They were all gone
in minutes!

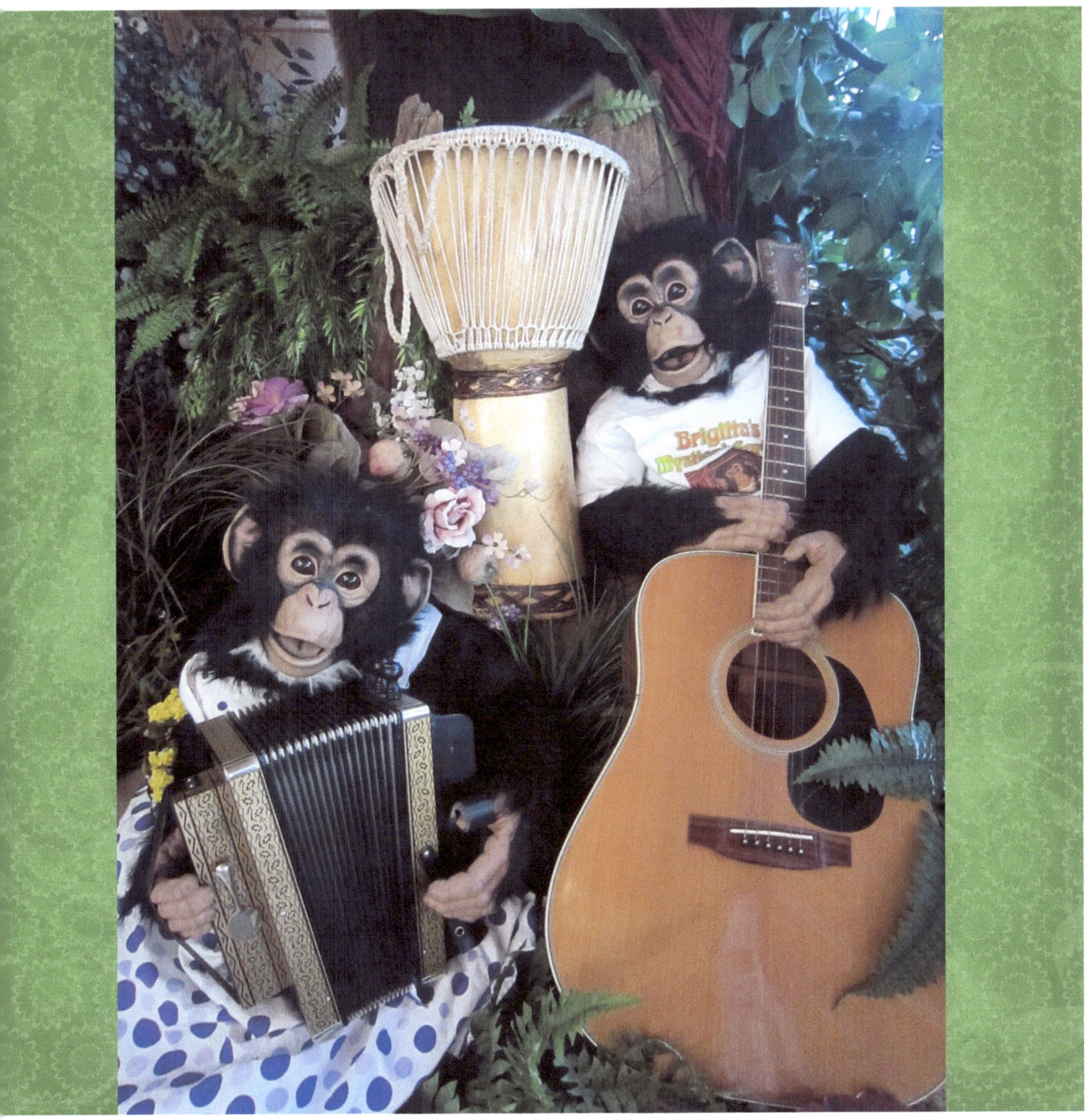

Keeping an even bigger secret from
his Mommy and Daddy,
Baby Bongo knew he gave
into temptation to be dishonest,
which took him onto a path
that will change his
chimpanzee life forever!

Thanks to Cliff-Flea, the flea, who
loves to leave sugary donuts behind.

Meanwhile Baby Bongo's parents
were still singing to the music
not noticing their little chimp
had tip-toed away.

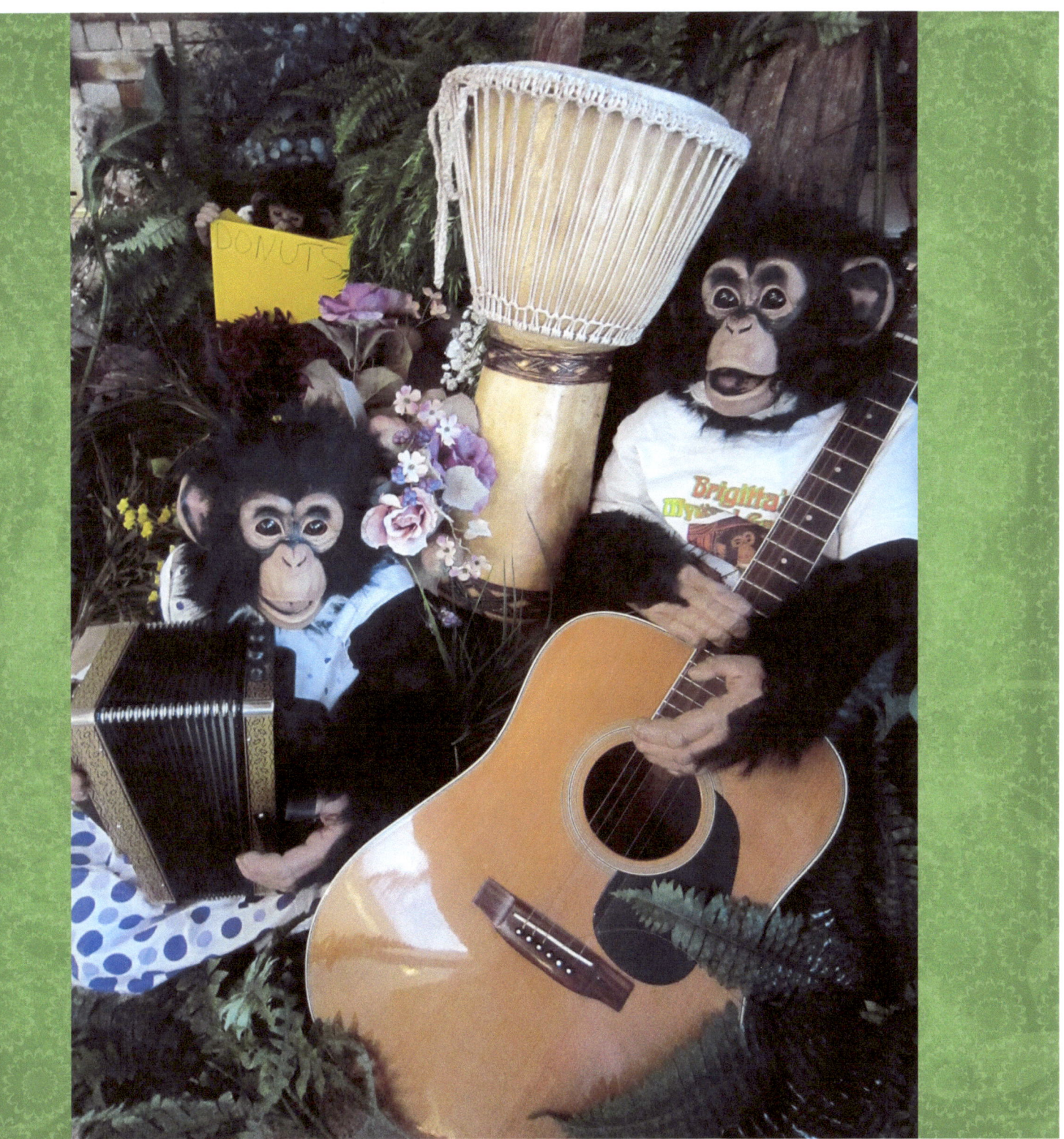

When Baby Bongo returned from his break, he started bing-ing and bong-ing all over the place!

At first his Mommy and Daddy were excited that Baby Bongo loved to play music!

Everyone was doing flips and flops celebrating the new Baby Bongo vibe, when suddenly Baby Bongo broke his instrument!

His parents knew right away that something was wrong!

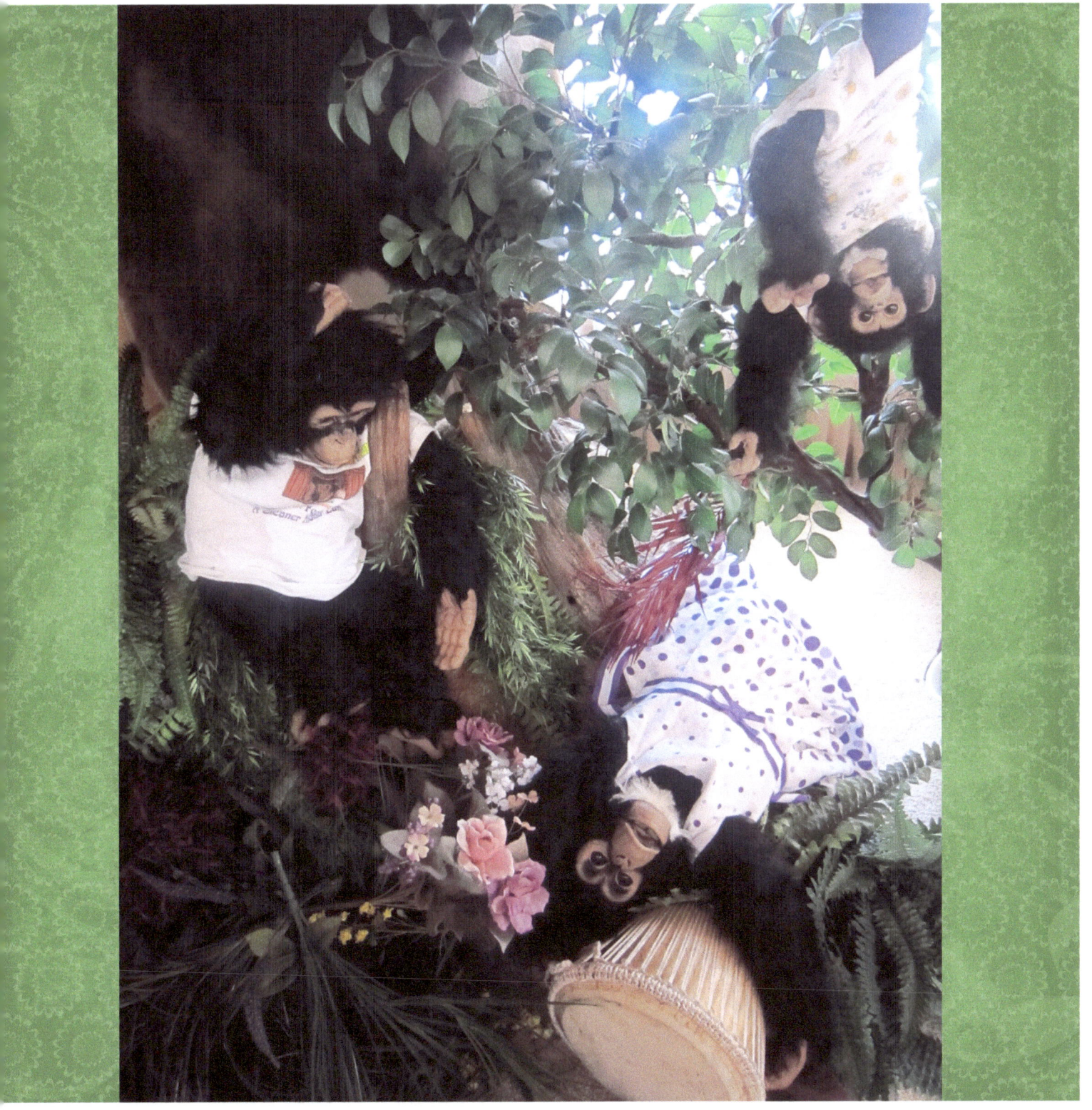

"No! Baby Bongo" his Father said,
"Although we are excited about your
new vibe, you must stay with
the positive one."

Baby Bongo's Mother agreed,
"You know it is very important to keep
your instrument clean and well-tuned,
or your instrument can break down,"
she hugged.

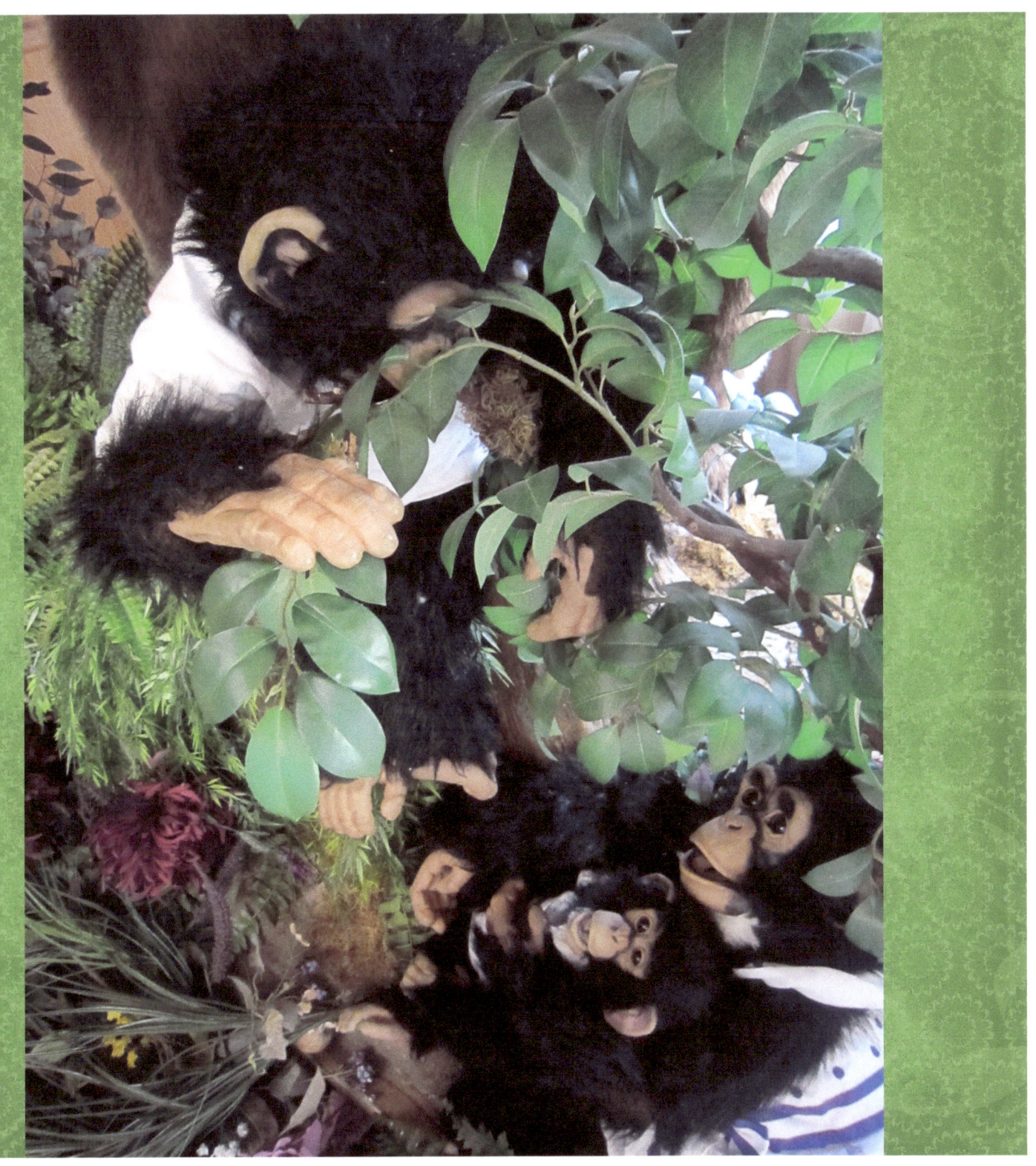

Baby Bongo did not care or want
to listen to his parents. In fact, he stuck
his tongue out at his Daddy, and told his
Mommy, "Na-Na-Naa-Boo Boooo!
You can't catch me!"

Marimba and Viola were in shock!

They took their little chimpanzee to the
vet immediately to find out why
Baby Bongo changed his behavior.

After all, Baby Bongo cherished
all musical instruments.

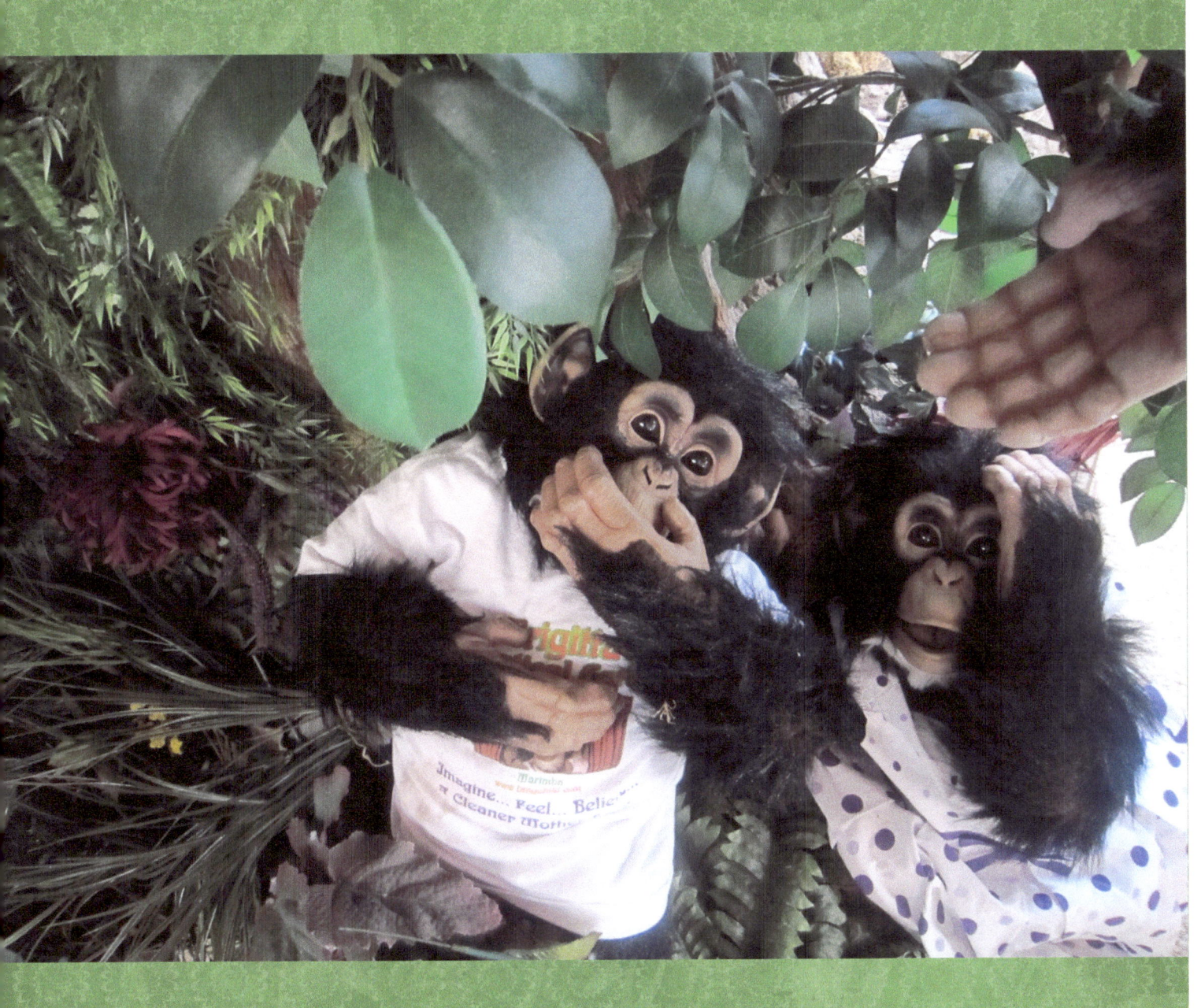

Baby Bongo's parents were right!
Dr. V-Vet found donuts all over
Baby Bongo's x-ray!

"Where on earth did Baby Bongo get all
these donuts?" the vet asked his parents.

Baby Bongo couldn't keep his secret any
longer and he told the truth to his
Mommy and Daddy.

"It looks like Baby Bongo ate a whole box!"
Marimba shook his head, "I think
Baby Bongo is allergic to
something in those donuts."

Viola leaps for the door "Marimba" she said,
"Let's go home now and find the empty box!
The ingredients will tell the whole story."

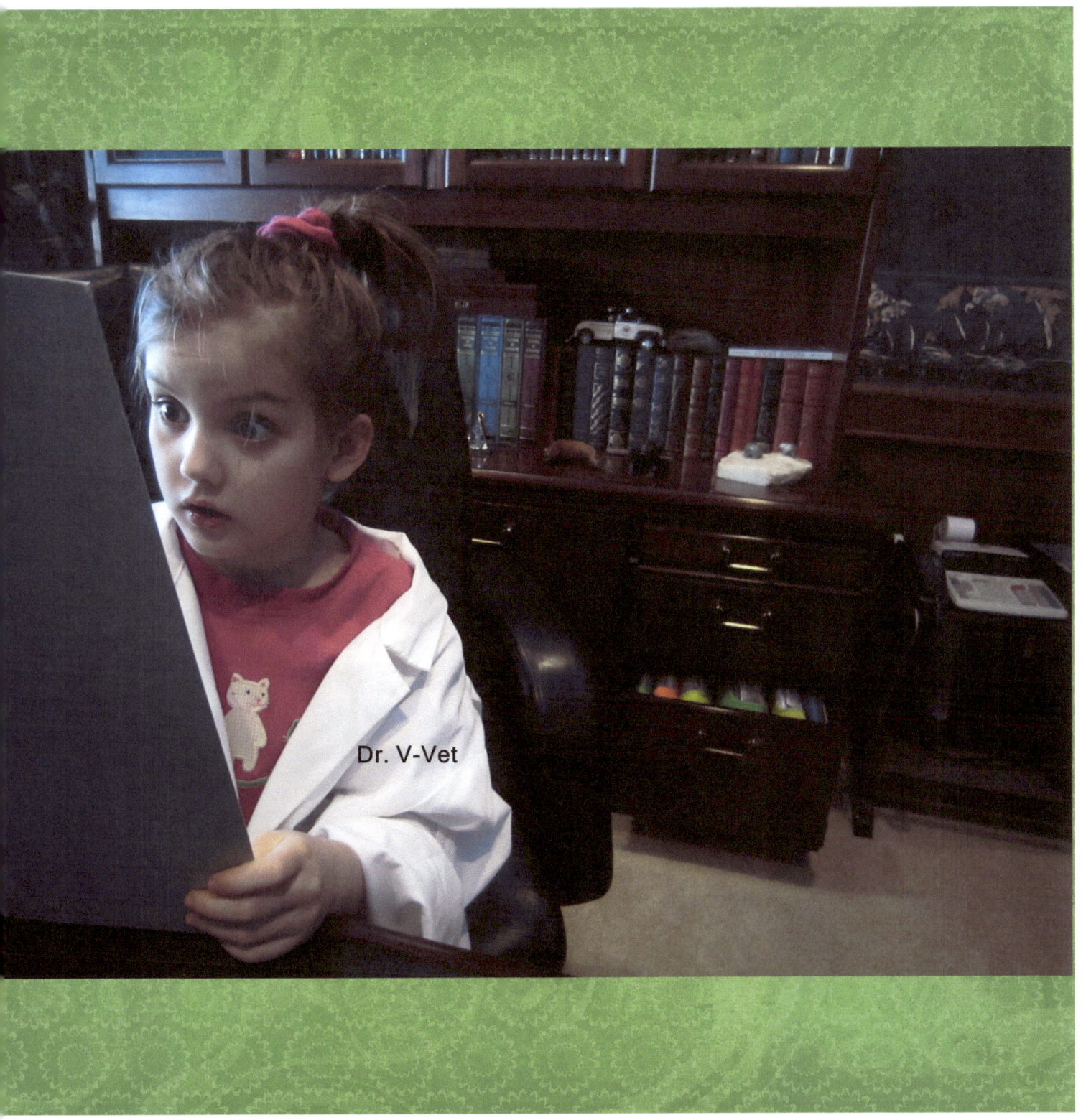

Dr. V-Vet

A week later and days of research
Dr.V-Vet found out that Baby Bongo
was allergic to unnatural sugars.

The vet told Marimba and Viola that
Baby Bongo could only
eat natural sugars from now on.

These are the sweets from God's
garden like apples and bananas;
no unnatural sugars, especially
unnatural donuts!

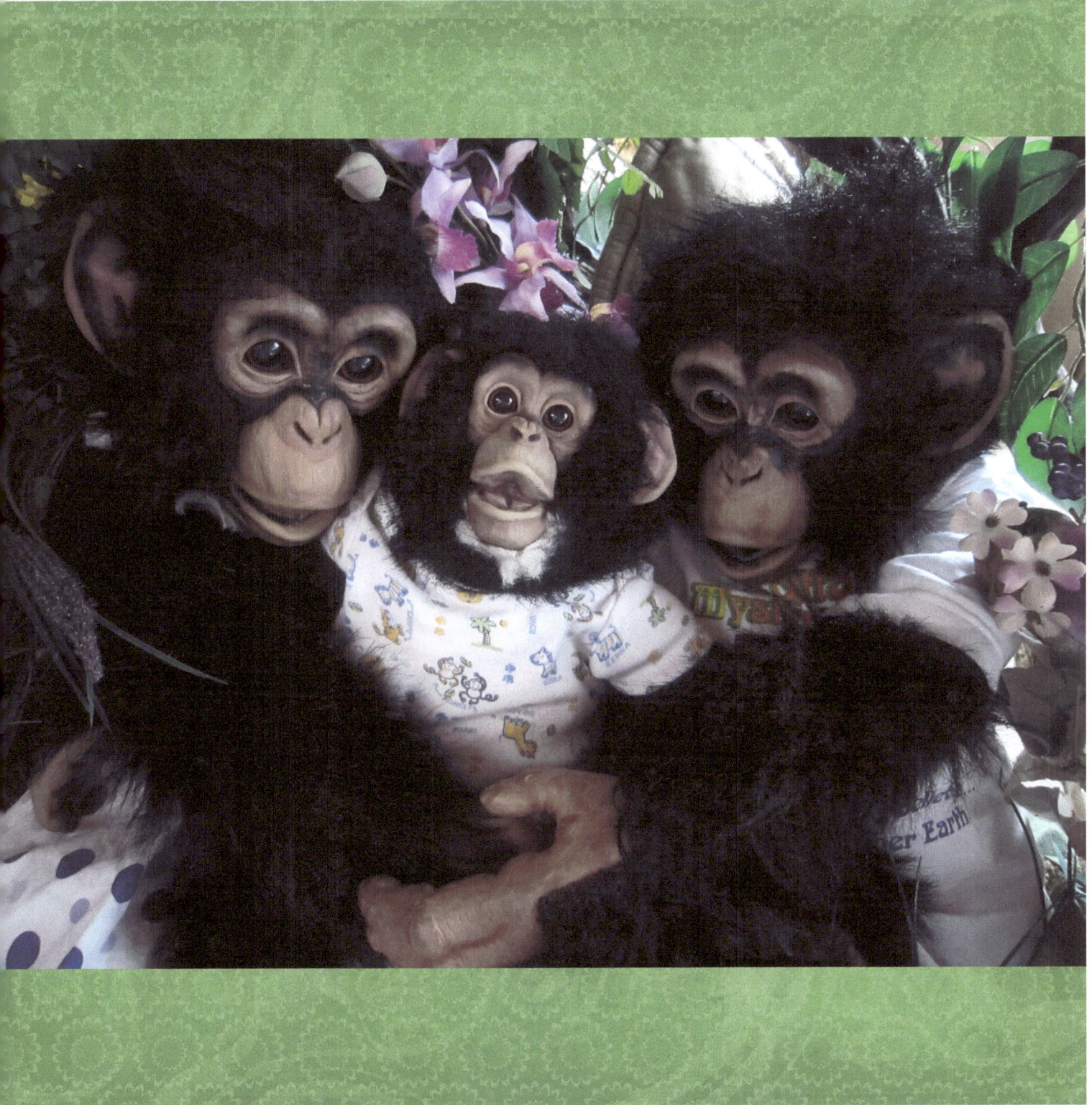

With the secret out, all was going well for Baby Bongo because he was eating only God's sugar.

Then he attended his best friend, Suzie's birthday party. Surprisingly a dish full of the sweetest, unnatural sweets were delivered by Cliff-Flea and his gang of biters.

They tempted everyone to join them to eat their unhealthy treats which included sugary donuts.

Baby Bongo was very tempted but his Mommy and Daddy quickly spoke to him.

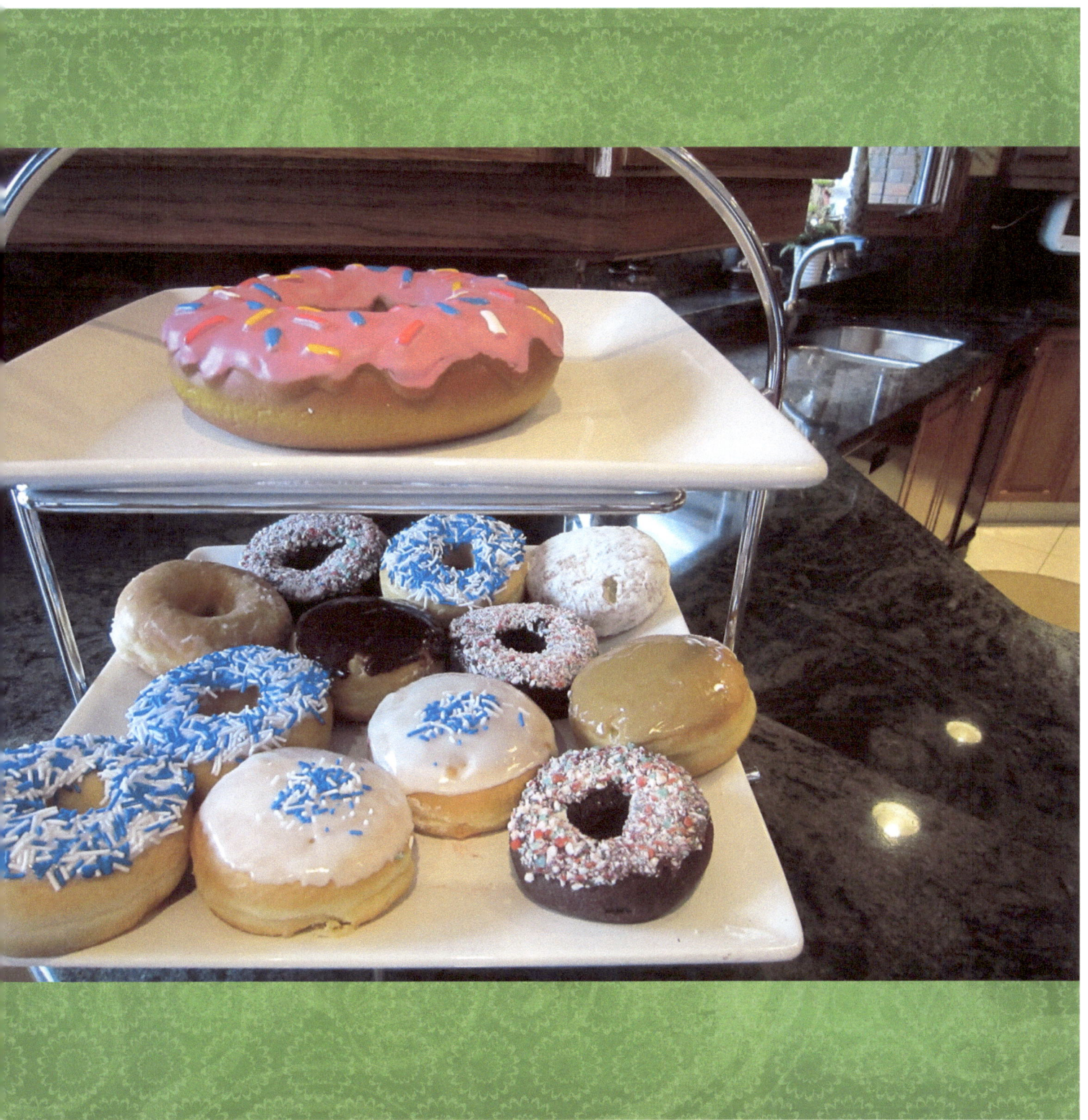

They told Baby Bongo,
"when you are tempted, take time to
pray for love and understanding and
you will be able to say no
to unnatural sugars."

Baby Bongo jumped away from the
sugary donuts and prayed.

Indeed his prayers were overflowing
with love and understanding.

Baby Bongo ate only from
the colorful fruit platter, until ...

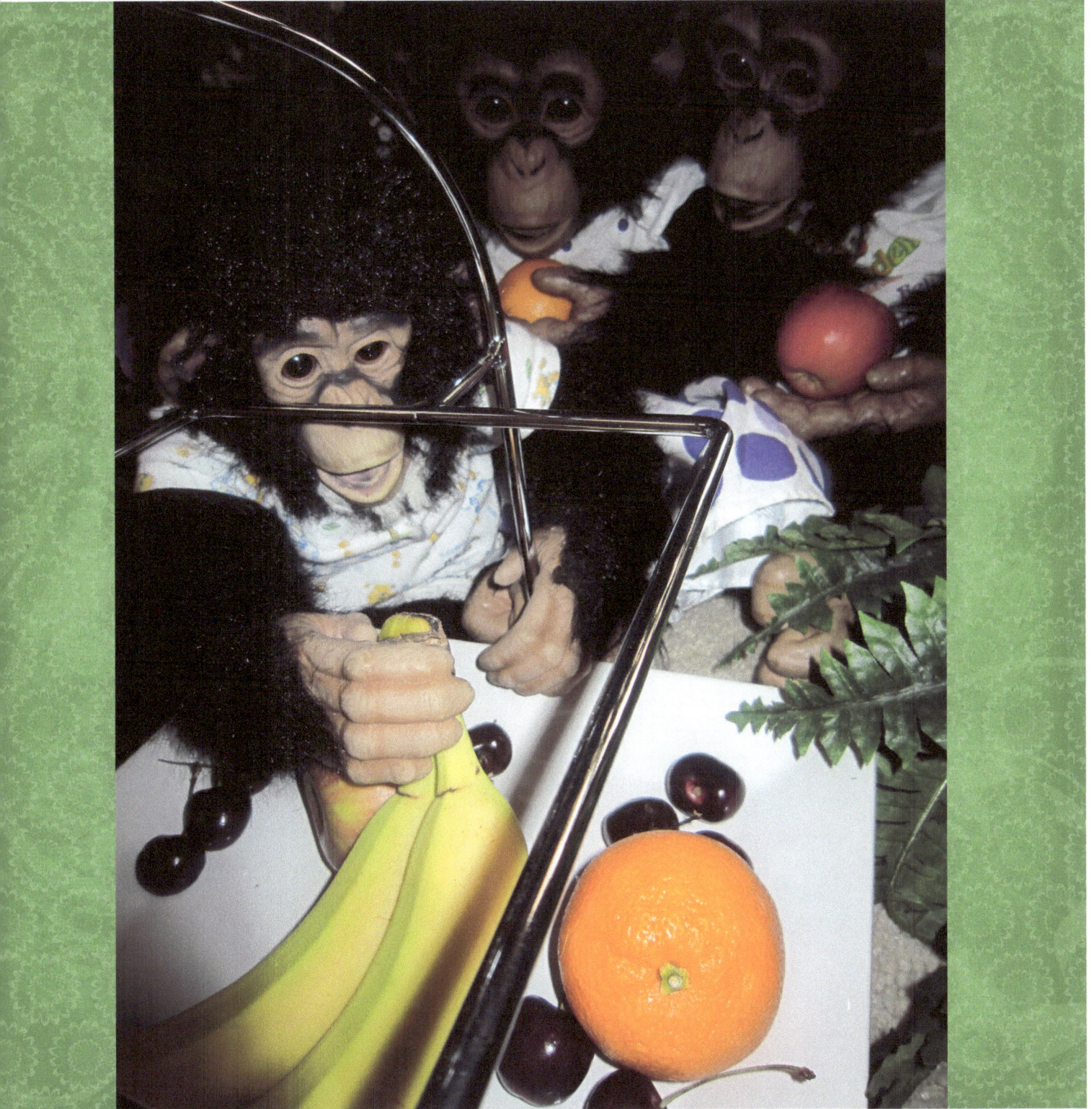

... he lost his focus!

Baby Bongo was distracted by one of Cliff-Flea's sweet treats rolling off the table and right out the window!

Not only did the sugary donut look so delicious but the donut could roll, and roll and roll.

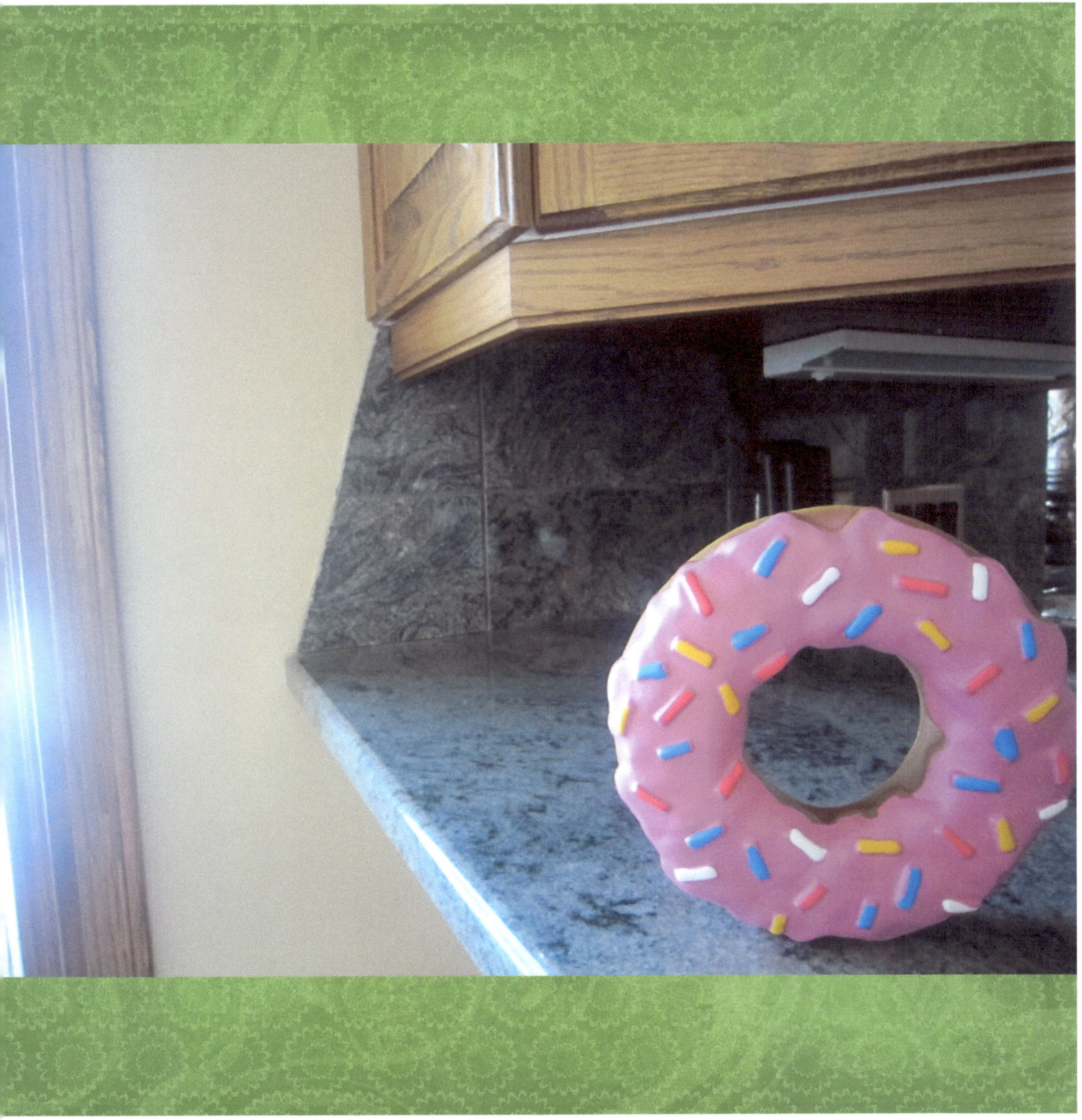

Marimba and Viola quickly
tried to stop Baby Bongo
from chasing the sugary donut
but Baby Bongo was faster and
chased the sugary donut outside
and deep into the jungle.

Marimba and Viola prayed
for help to find Baby Bongo safe.

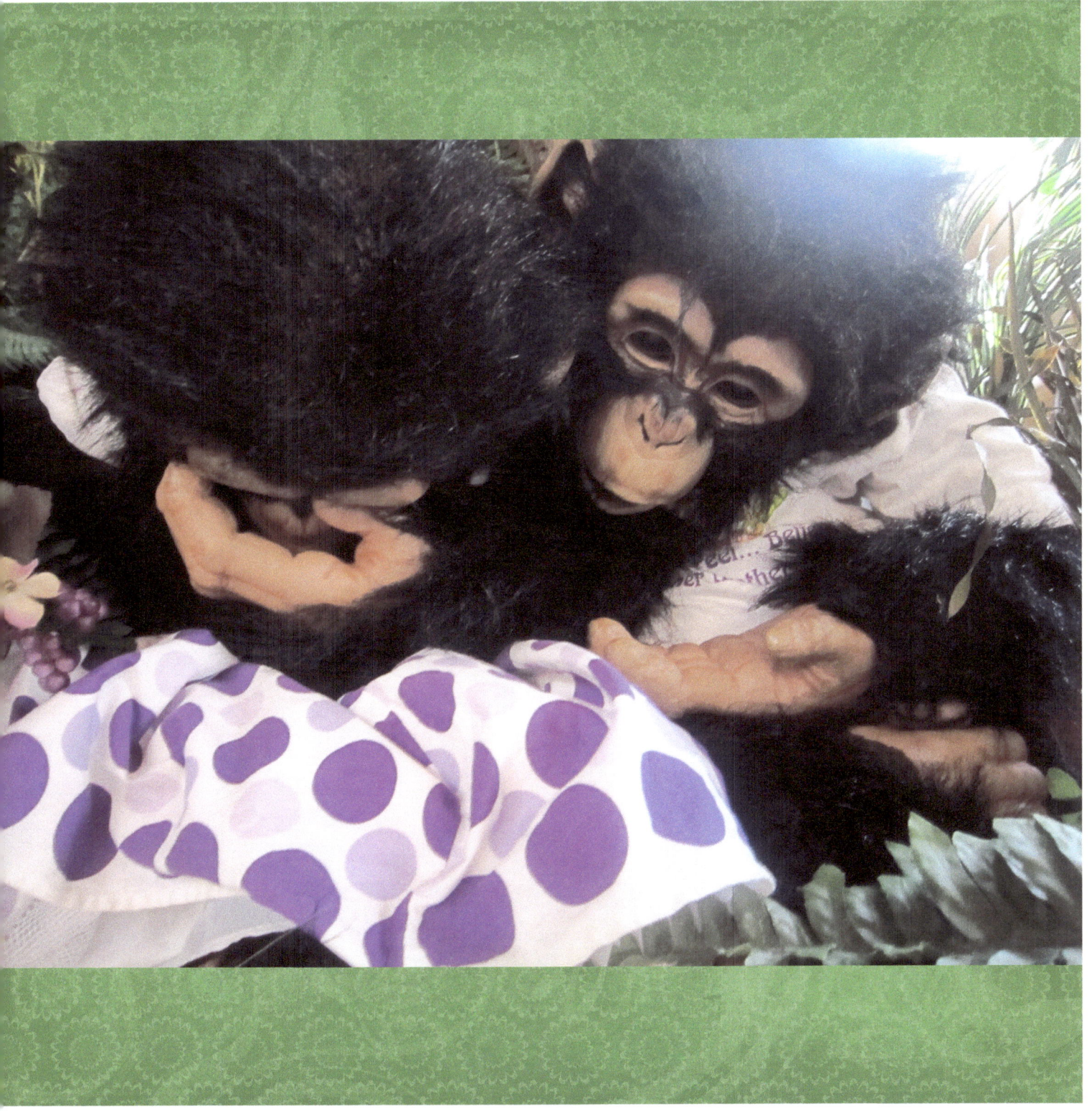

Alone and far in the jungle,
Baby Bongo was face to face
with the sugary donut.

Temptation never
looked sweeter!

With a spark, Cliff-Flea and his
flea gang showed up surrounding
the innocent Baby Bongo,
chanting

"Eat the sweet!
Eat the sweet!
Eat the sweet!"

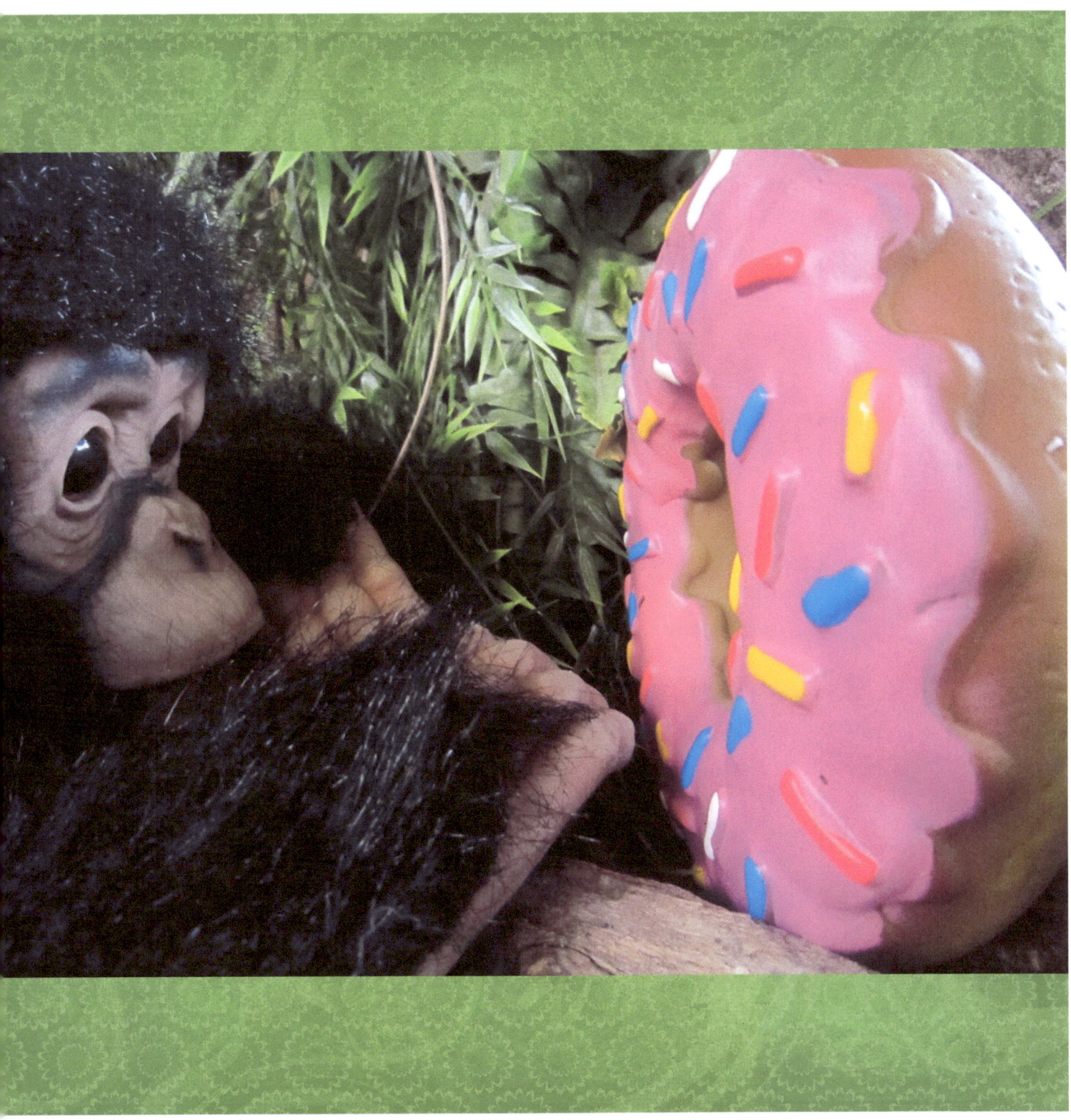

Baby Bongo could not turn away
from the donut. It looked so good
with pink icing and sparkly sprinkles!

"Baby Bongo", his mother softly cried out
but Baby Bongo could not see
his Mommy!

Tempted to take the first bite,
Baby Bongo heard
his Father's strong voice saying,
"Do the right thing, Baby Bongo,
even if no one can see you."

But he could not see his
Father anywhere, either.

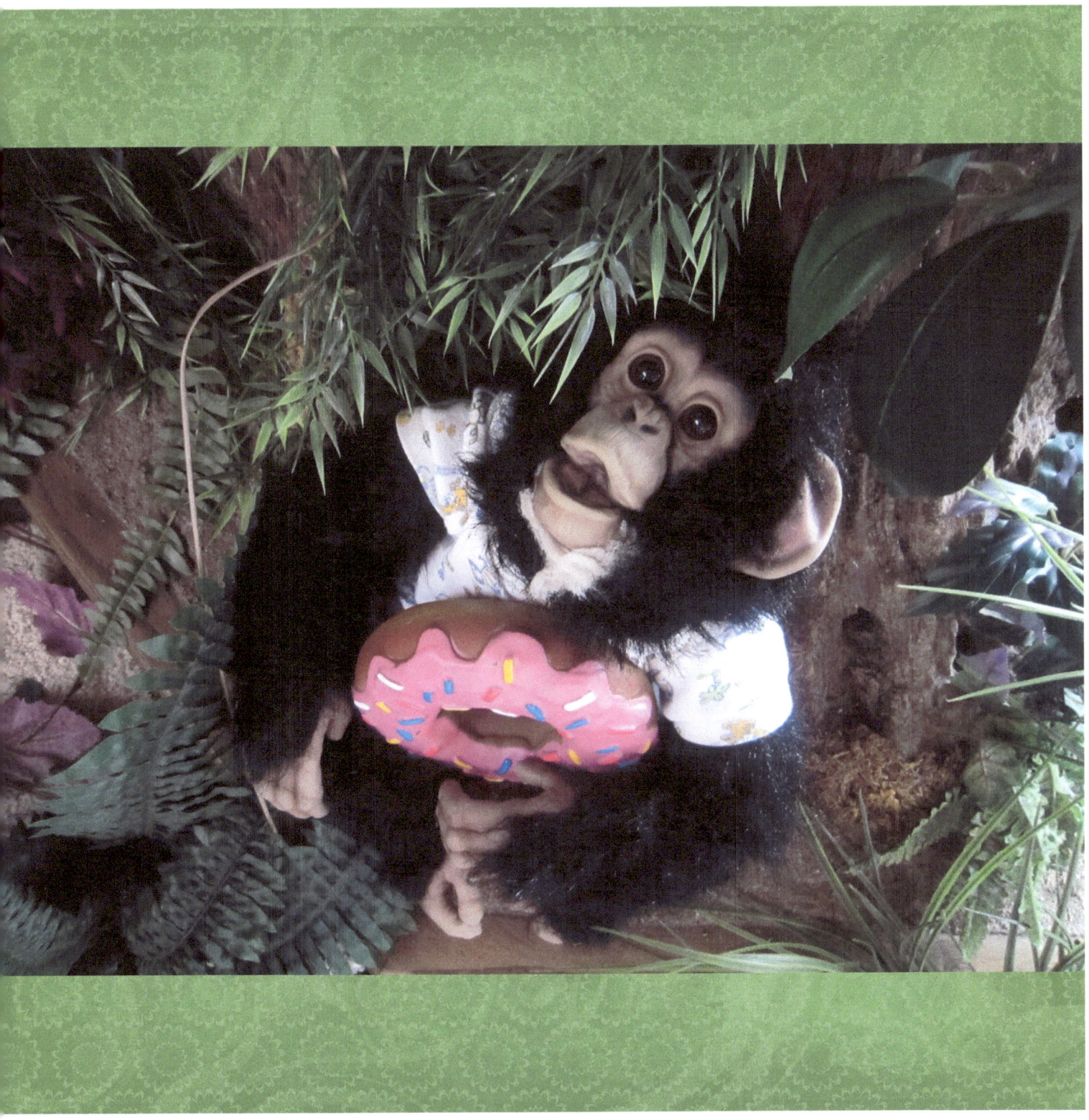

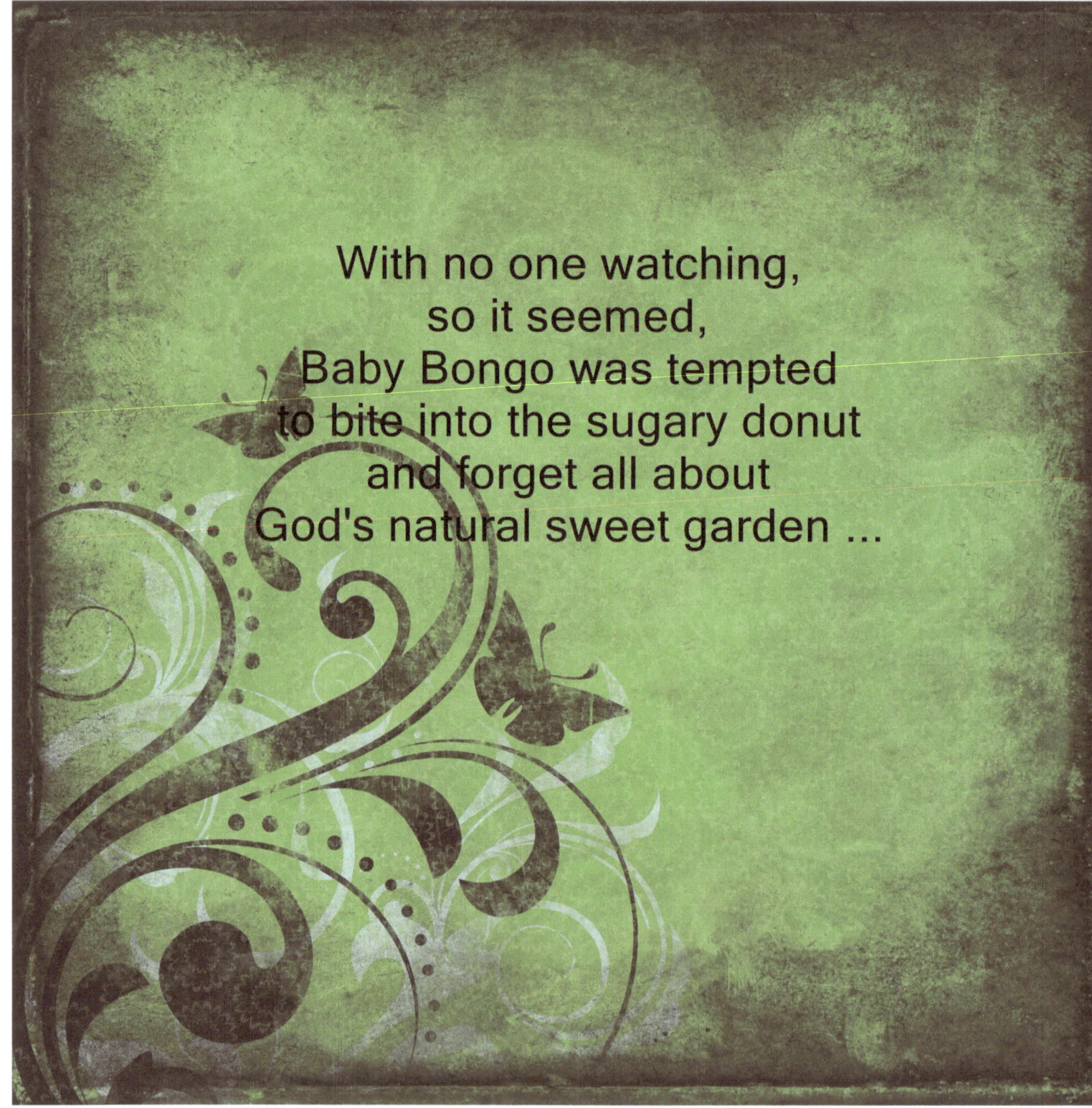

With no one watching,
so it seemed,
Baby Bongo was tempted
to bite into the sugary donut
and forget all about
God's natural sweet garden ...

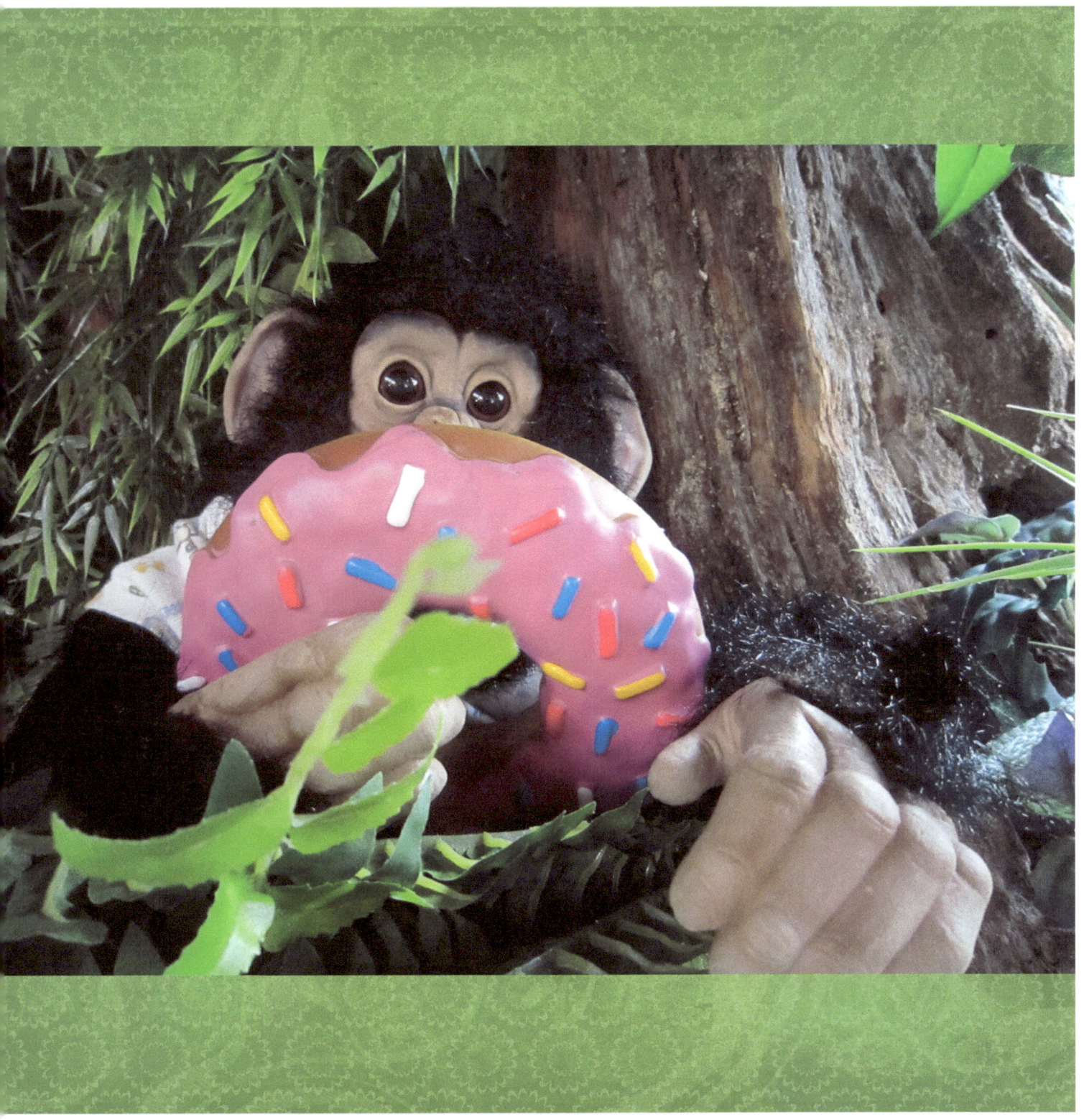

... when suddenly Baby Bongo
remembered about
the power of prayer.

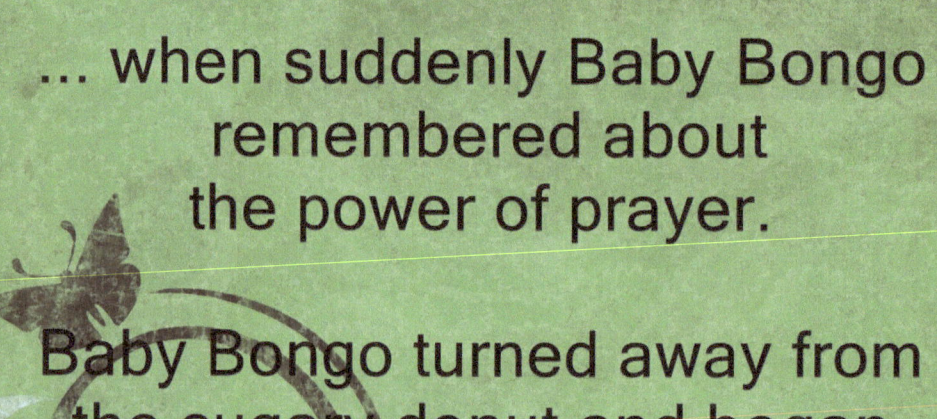

Baby Bongo turned away from
the sugary donut and began
to pray for help!

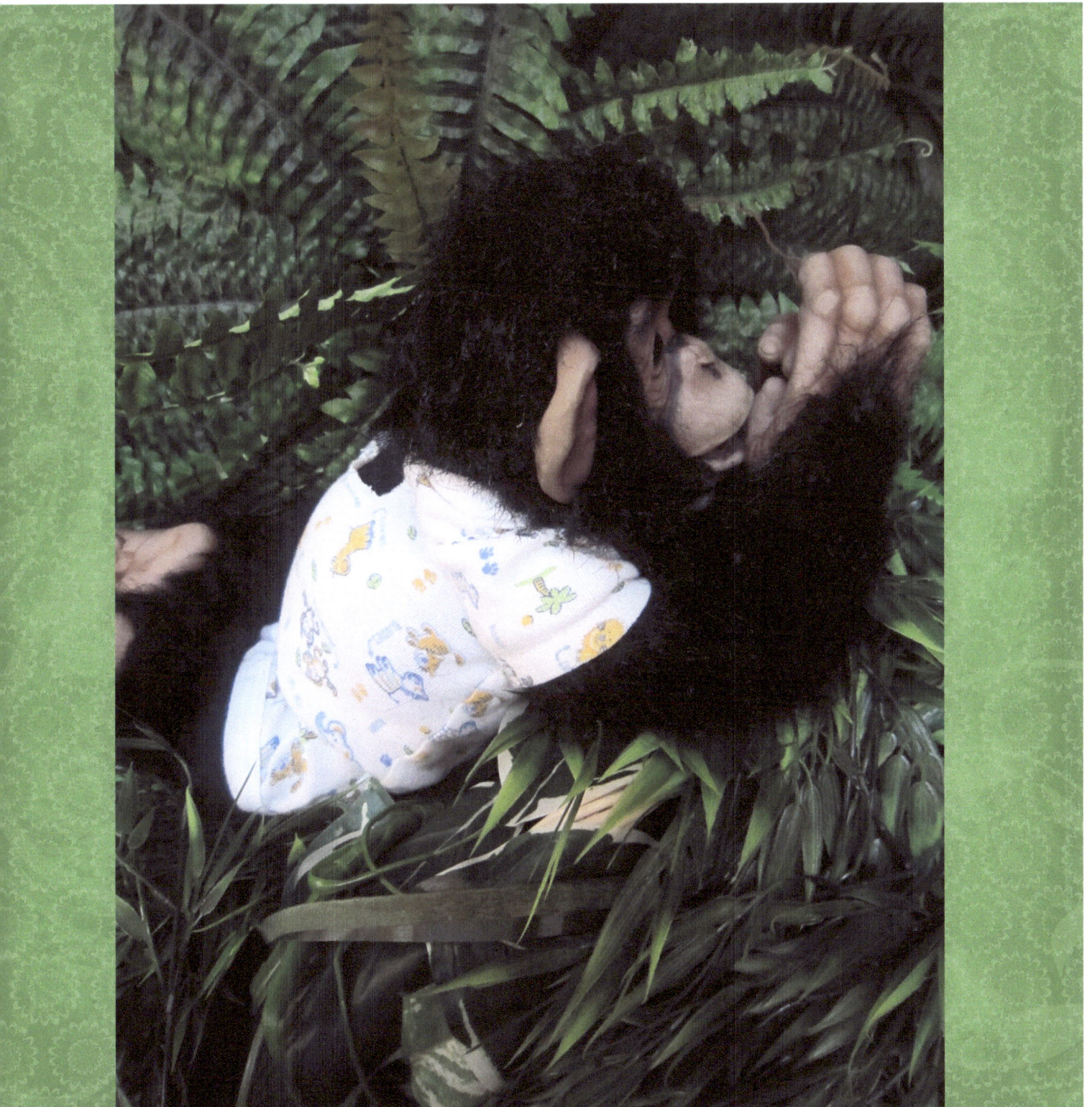

Cliff-Flea and his gang
screamed in horror,
witnessing their unnatural plan
going right down the drain.

They heard Baby Bongo praying
for the courage to be
a healthy chimpanzee and
to stay away from unnatural sugar.

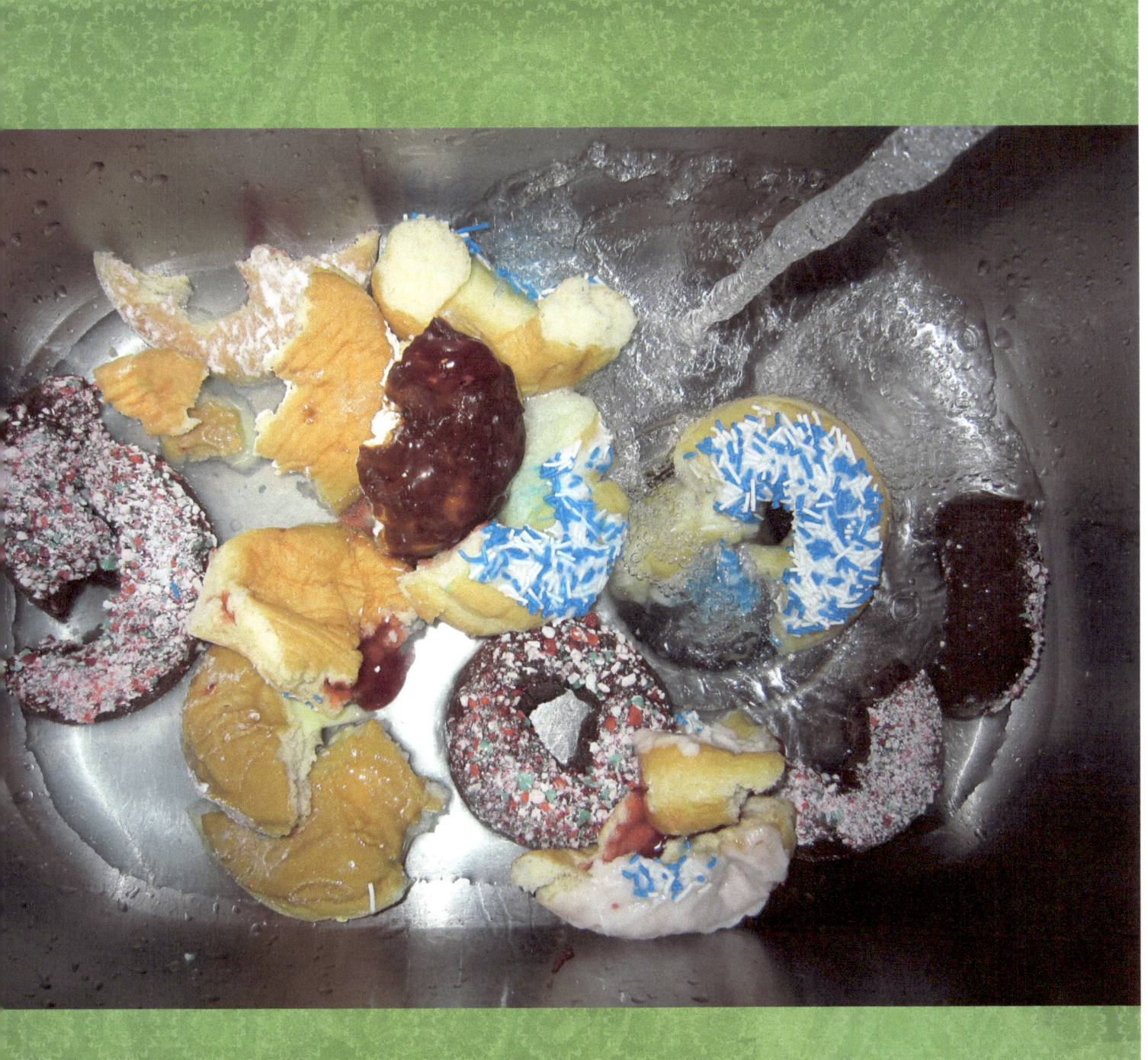

Suddenly, Baby Bongo's Mommy and Daddy arrived with big hugs for their little chimpanzee.

They were delighted that Baby Bongo prayed to God to help him avoid the temptation of unnatural sugar and for the courage to say no!

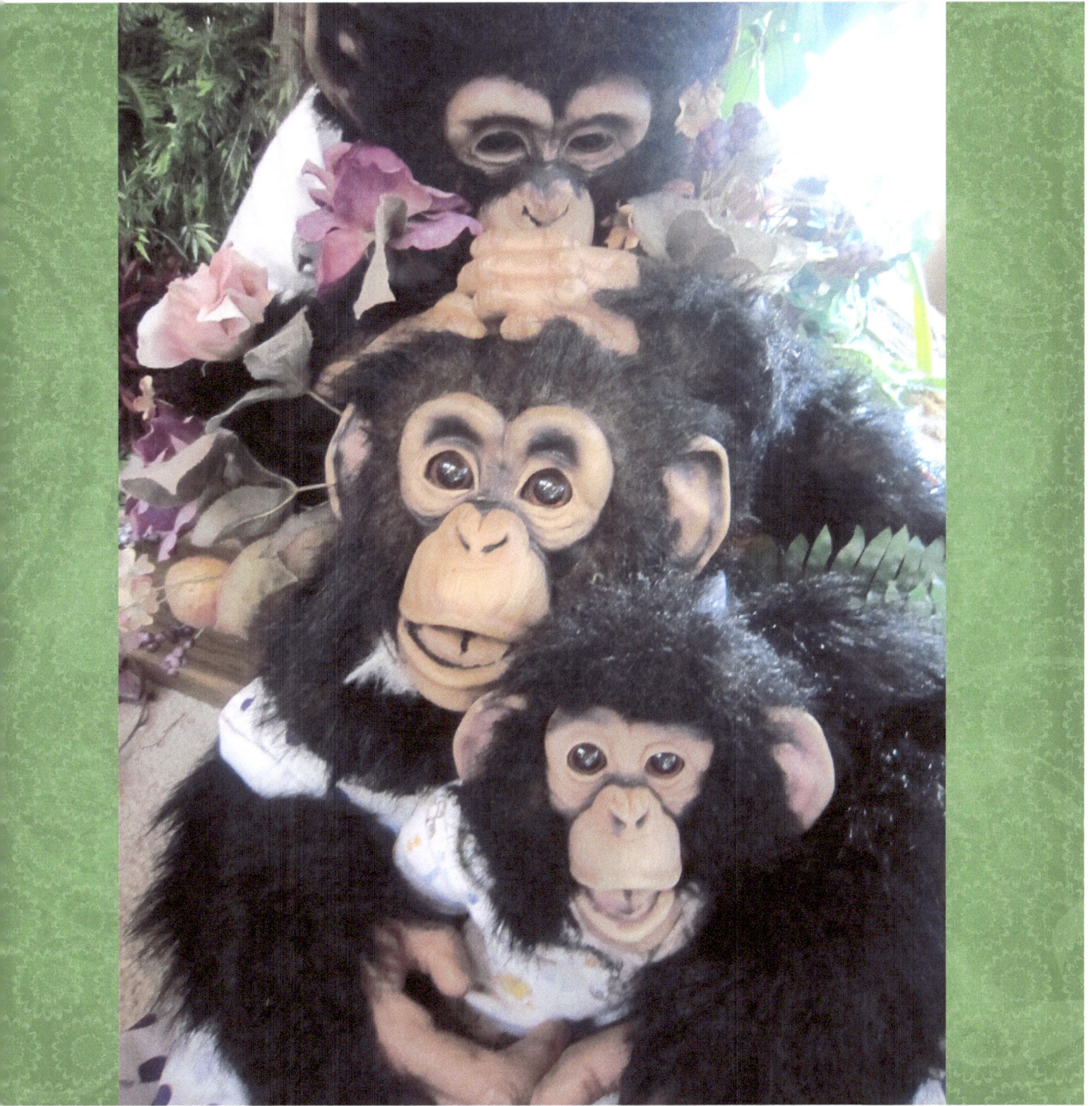

Later that evening, Baby Bongo
talked with his Mommy and Daddy.

He told them how he was tempted,
and how prayer supported him to do
what is right and true.

Marimba and Viola smiled.

They both knew faith and prayer
would help Baby Bongo swing
on the healthy vine again.

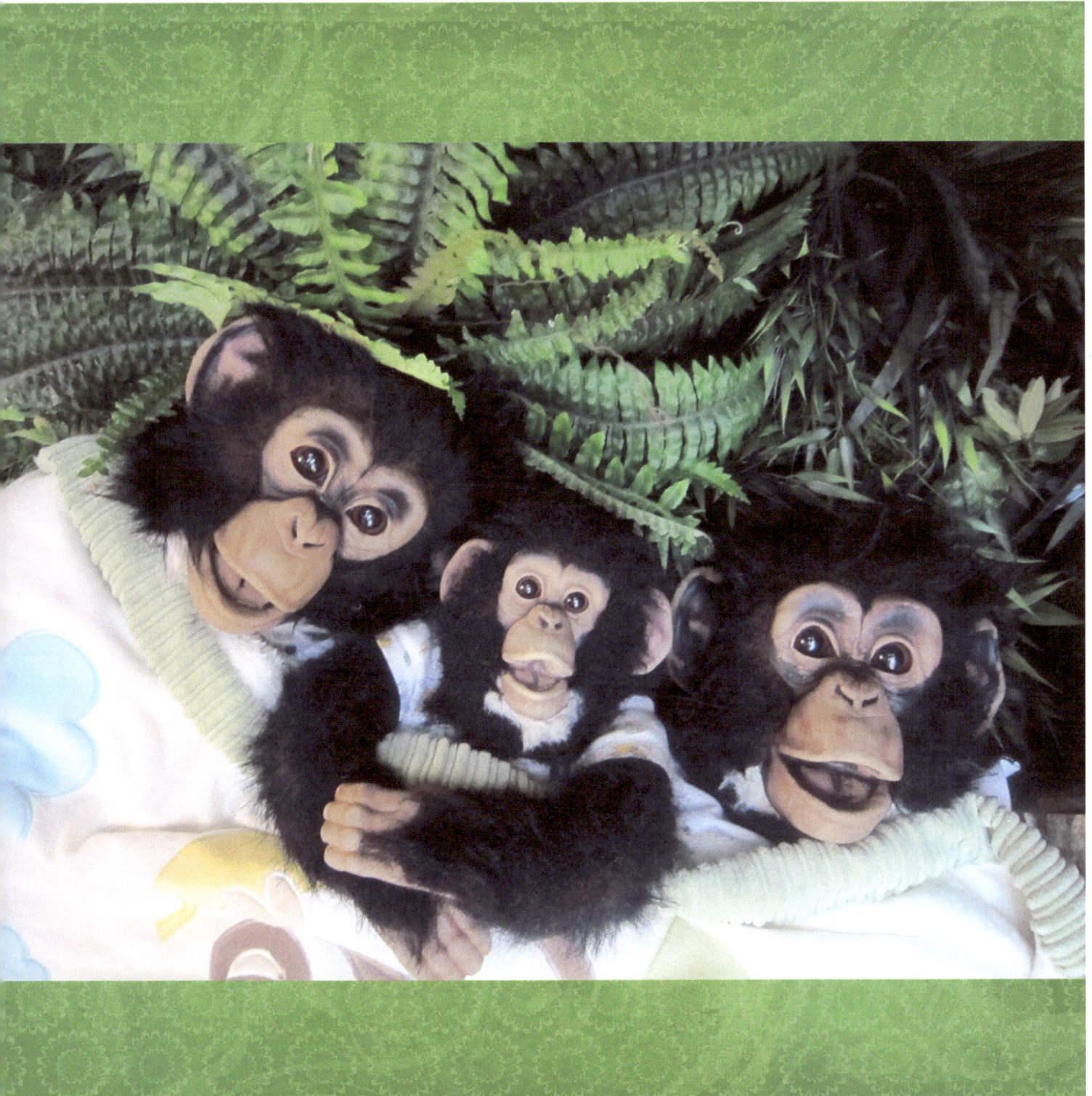